Bibliographic information published by the German National Library:

The German National Library lists this publication in the National Bibliography; detailed bibliographic data are available on the Internet at http://dnb.dnb.de .

Imprint:

Copyright © 2002 GRIN Verlag, Open Publishing GmbH
Print and binding: Books on Demand GmbH, Norderstedt Germany
ISBN: 9783668367210

This book at GRIN:

http://www.grin.com/en/e-book/347165/the-western-doctrine-of-reincarnation-a-critique-from-the-point-of-view

Frank Drescher

The Western Doctrine of Reincarnation. A Critique From the Point of View of Catholic Theology

GRIN Publishing

GRIN - Your knowledge has value

Since its foundation in 1998, GRIN has specialized in publishing academic texts by students, college teachers and other academics as e-book and printed book. The website www.grin.com is an ideal platform for presenting term papers, final papers, scientific essays, dissertations and specialist books.

Visit us on the internet:

http://www.grin.com/

http://www.facebook.com/grincom

http://www.twitter.com/grin_com

Frank Drescher

The western doctrine of reincarnation – a critique from the point of view of Catholic theology

1. Introduction

In this contribution[1] I am not looking for confrontation with those who believe in a doctrine of reincarnation. Nor do I want to be a dogmatic know-all or the kind of person who superciliously dismisses the faith-context of two world religions (i.e., Hinduism and Buddhism). Today's Catholic theology is sincerely seeking a respectful and peaceable dialogue with the different religions – and the recently canonized Pope John Paul II repeatedly showed this by his own example – so that people might be able to live together in peace, tolerance and mutual understanding throughout the world, but also, and particularly, in our own multicultural and multi-religious society. Whenever dogma has been made the subject of dispute between people it has ended in violence and blood-letting. Decades ago, consequently, Catholic theologians (at least the overwhelming majority of them) abandoned disputes on matters of faith with people outside the Catholic ambit. Catholic Christians have had to learn bitter lessons from their past mistakes and now prefer open dialogue to embittered confrontation. The Second Vatican Council committed itself to this approach in the following words :

The Catholic Church rejects nothing that is true and holy in these religions. She regards with sincere reverence those ways of conduct and of life, those precepts and teachings which, though differing in many aspects from the ones she holds and sets forth, nonetheless often reflect a ray of that Truth which enlightens all men. [....] The Church, therefore, exhorts her sons, that through dialogue and collaboration with the followers of other religions, carried out with prudence and love and in witness to the Christian faith and life, they recognize, preserve and promote the good things, spiritual and moral, as well as the socio-cultural values found among these men.

Nostra aetate 2

Explicity, what I am offering is a clear, positive statement of the Christian faith itself, which has been increasingly called into question in our society in recent decades. Unfortunately this questioning goes hand-in-hand with a (by now) widespread religious indifference on the part even of those of our fellow-citizens who regard themselves – in the broadest sense – as adherents of the Christian religion. My critique is therefore quite deliberately addressed to

---

[1] A slightly reworked and updated version of a lecture given on 12.01.2002 at the XLVI. Weekend Conference of the Philosophical Institute of the RWTH Aachen under Prof.Dr.V.Berning entitled "Über die Seele III: Weltseele – Seelenwanderung – Parapsychologie" in the Arnold Janssen Monastery, Wahlwiller, Netherlands.

those within the Christian fold who would attempt to fabricate a western-style syncretizing version of the doctrine of reincarnation and amalgamate it with Christian convictions.

2. Reincarnation – a question for Christian theology ?

There is a recurring legend to the effect that in early Christianity there were believers in reincarnation who were subsequently wiped out by the Church's official theology. This legend keeps cropping up. In fact it flies in the face of the historical facts and cannot be found in the sources at all.

In the Early Church not a single Christian theologian can be found to have defended the idea that the dead assume a new embodiment. Such a belief would have been meaningless, given the apostolic faith as transmitted in the ancient Church. Rather, theologians at that time were busy refuting gnosticism, a many-sided, syncretistic religious movement of late antiquity that, with roots in Platonism, taught a reincarnation of the dead. (An example of this is Manichaeism, which posed a real challenge, if not an actual threat, to early Christianity even as late as the 5th/6th centuries – a period when the Catholic Church was gradually taking shape.) The Church Fathers and other theologians of the ancient Church never regarded this doctrine of reincarnation as a Christian teaching. It was not even held to be a heresy, which would have had to be condemned. It was always seen as a non-Christian belief, and the Church has never officially condemned beliefs that are external to itself. Why should it ?

Origen is occasionally cited as a proponent of reincarnation. He was one of the Church Fathers of the 3rd century and was held in such high regard that, even in the 5th century, Christian theologians argued about his views and condemned some of his teachings. However, Origen taught only the pre-existence of souls, a doctrine that was definitively rejected by the universal Church at the time.

The doctrine of reincarnation has only gained prominence in present theological debate :

- **Karl Rahner** regards the doctrine of reincarnation as a possible starting-point for a more acceptable interpretation of the Church's problematical teaching on the soul's intermediate state (between death and resurrection); it would function as a kind of replacement for Purgatory.
- **Hans Küng** wonders whether the doctrine of reincarnation, like other teachings in the history of theology (e.g., those that arose in a Hellenistic context), could be

integrated into the Christian system of teaching and faith as a means of promoting an ecumenism of world religions.

- **Michael von Brück** sees the doctrine of reincarnation, in the context of dialogue with the eastern religions, as a starting-point in the search for a solution to the problem of the theodicy and as a model for explaining the "irrationality of the universe".

From the perspective of historico-biblical studies and systematic theology none of these three approaches can be validated, as I shall show in the following section.

Nonetheless, despite these serious issues Catholic theology does acknowledge certain common elements between the eastern doctrine of reincarnation and the Christian faith :

- Both faith-systems embrace a hope that goes beyond death and transcends a purely materialistic world-view.
- We also share the conviction that the actions of human beings have consequences even beyond death.
- We counter all fatalism by insisting on man's moral responsibility for his own life and its fulfilment.
- We share a belief that the individual's life is woven into the past history of mankind.
- We also share the belief in the individual's ethical purification, a process that is not simply ended by death, but leads man towards his fulfilment.

Having said this, overwhelming differences remain between the two world-views, and for this reason the two religious conceptions of man's fulfilment in and/or after death cannot consistently be reconciled.

3. Reasons why the doctrine of reincarnation is theologically incompatible with the Christian faith

First, some words of clarification before we examine in detail why the two world-views under consideration are incompatible. Theologically speaking it is *irrelevant* whether there is actually a body of Christians who have combined the doctrine of reincarnation with their personal faith and woven it into their religious conceptions. In our society, for instance, there are people who do not accept the doctrine of the Trinity, or the divinity and incarnation of

Christ, or his resurrection after his death on the cross, and yet still call themselves Christians.

As far as the Catholic Church is concerned, however, being a Christian is not (only) a matter of how one describes oneself; it depends crucially on whether one shares in the Christian community of faith and tradition – even if such a view is unpopular in our emphatically tolerant and pluralist society (that is also, alas! indifferent and undiscerning). Moreover, this ecclesiastically constituted community proclaims *without any doubt* and *from its very origins* that any kind of doctrine of reincarnation, of whatever provenance, is absolutely incompatible with its fundamental convictions. It does this on the basis of its Jewish roots and its biblical faith in the resurrection, handed on from the apostles and their successors, and written for all time into the Christian confession of faith that validly binds all the major Churches and ecclesial communities. The Christian faith, after all, has its own profile that cannot be altered or watered-down.

One often hears the frivolous objection that the doctrine of reincarnation has never been rejected and condemned as erroneous by the Church's teaching office. As we have said, non-Christian convictions do not need to be evaluated or condemned by the Church's magisterium unless they are put forward as Christian teachings or as compatible with them.

The fundamental reasons for the incompatibility of the two world-views are the following:

- **The Christian belief in Creation.** All that exists in the world is Creation, willed by God as such and called into being by him. This applies particularly to the human soul, which therefore cannot be held to be "divine" in any way. The soul receives its immortality from God: it does not have immortality *of its own nature*. Our souls were never a part of God and so there is no question of them *returning* to him to be reunited with him, as is claimed by some dualistic world-views of largely gnostic origin.

  The immortality promised to us is something given: its origin is in God's deep, unconditional love that is firmly covenanted to us and therefore cannot be lost. We are immortal because God loves us with an undying love, in our personality and individuality, and affirms each of us as an utterly concrete "Thou"

  Our soul is the human organ of communication between man and God, whereby we open to his care for us and respond to it. That is what makes us loved and

5

affirmed by God, not some supposed divine origin on the part of our soul. Here, in the genuinely *Christian understanding of God and man,* we have an unbridgeable chasm that separates us from any form of reincarnation doctrine.

- **Fulfilment and forgiveness.** Some proponents of reincarnation assert that this doctrine is an adequate replacement for the Catholic teaching on Purgatory and, incidentally, could also solve the problem of man's "intermediate" status between death and resurrection. This is categorically rejected by Roman Catholic theology, together with Orthodox and Protestant theology, even if individual theologians from these Churches or ecclesial communities express views of this kind.

  The Christian faith takes this life seriously; the individual life-history of each human being is a *one-off opportunity,* including all his decisions right up to his death. Our faith trusts that God will accept us when we die, just as we are, just as we have developed, with our whole life as we have lived it, including the personal guilt with which we have burdened ourselves. And we believe that the final, ultimate meeting with God's mercy and love after our death will have a transforming and purifying effect.

  We must be aware of our sinfulness, however; we must deal with it, repent of it and be prepared to accept it, just as we accept God's mercy. This contrition, conditioned by the experience of our failure in the face of God's pure truth and love, is a thoroughly painful process, but one that brings about and perfects the person's purification. God's forgiveness and our own "salvation" are not things we can produce by our own power, even if we had a thousand lives to live (according to the old proverb, "The word that helps you is not the one you speak"); for this we need the saving work of Christ, for only God himself is in a position to span the infinite gulf between the Creator and the sinful creature. In view of these considerations and a whole succession of failed theological tentatives of this kind, there is no room for man's self-redemption, not even by a succession of reincarnations.

- **The resurrection of the body.** The Christian conviction is that man is fundamentally constituted as body-and-soul. This excludes any kind of dualism, which is unthinkable, particularly given our Jewish roots. In this context the body is more than mere material. As understood by biblical theology it is the one body that has gone through our entire life-history and through which we are in contact with our surroundings. This contact is effected *only* by our body. It is not merely or simply a miserable shell (or even an evil one) that imprisons a divine core, as is suggested, among others, by Platonism in all its variations.

Just as our soul is the organ whereby we relate to God, our body is the organ whereby we relate to the world and to our fellow-men. It is the body that enables us to live in relationships, to love and suffer, and so it profoundly shapes our identity as human beings. It follows that the body cannot simply be sloughed off and replaced by a new one. This concrete body is an *essential* constituent part of the human being, of his individuality and personality.

When man is promised salvation, it is something that applies to the *whole* human being; man does not *have* a body and a soul: he *is* body and soul.

The body is indissolubly bound up with our personal being; this means that, as persons, we will experience eternity in a body-and-soul mode. We draw this faith and hope from the bodily resurrection of Christ as it is attested by the apostles and as it is promised to us too: "Today you will be with me in paradise" - and not, in other words, after a long succession of rebirths.

As Christians we oppose "reincarnationism", and we do so on the basis of the following positive convictions:

- The personal, Triune God is the ground of our hope, not some faceless world system to which all living things are subordinated.
- Man is challenged to be an active subject; but his justification, purification and fulfillment in and after this earthly life are above all a grace and gift of the One God.
- History is linear, and is directed towards a goal. It is not cyclic. This goal is the perfection of existence in God.
- This goal is not the soul's liberation from the body, nor the human being's liberation from this world. Rather, it is the redemption of man, body and soul, and his fulfillment in and with this world, which is the affirmed and "good" creation of

the good God.

- This life is not merely a trial run or testing-ground; it is a unique opportunity with a meaning for salvation.

4.   Concluding remarks

Having tried to show why the Christian faith cannot in any way be linked with a doctrine of reincarnation, I would like to conclude, in line with the topic of our conference, with a few philosophical and ethical reservations regarding the doctrine of the reincarnation of the dead.

As an adherent of a religion of revelation (and as a committed "exoteric" in contrast to the "esoterics") I see an epistemological problem regarding the origins of the doctrine of reincarnation and of the cosmology that must undergird it.

Surely our philosophical insights speak against any form of esoteric knowledge? Whence might come this knowledge, arising in human beings and leading them to illumination? Do not such ideas, largely unsubstantiated by evidence, expose those who hold them to the suspicion of illusions and myth-making?

Is it not the case that the western notions of reincarnation (but by no means the eastern!) owe their existence to the widespread and completely understandable desire to make the most of this life and hopefully evolve to the highest degree of "self-realization"? And if that should not be entirely possible in this life, then possibly in the next, or the next-but-one! Is it not *this* that exercises the particular attraction for our western, entertainment-seeking and consumption-orientated "fun society", into which we Central Europeans are increasingly developing?

What meaning can history have nowadays in the face of a more or less "eternal recurrence" (Nietzsche!)? And is there not a danger that the doctrine of reincarnation could make us fail to take this life as seriously and responsibly as we should, given the the unique opportunity that it is? Why should I take the trouble to live my life at a meaningful level, orientated to a higher goal, if I can do this in a later life? These reasons alone show that reincarnation is not an adequate substitution for the Catholic Purgatory.

Finally, does not the doctrine of reincarnation lead to a certain cynicism vis-à-vis those who suffer, and, logically even vis-à-vis the Shoah? Why should we combat suffering, poverty and sickness if they are the self-inflicted consequences of the relevant karma or dharma, this faceless, implacable law of retributive causality? In my view this represents a very unsatisfactory "solution" to the problem of the theodicy.

The Christian faith shows itself here to be more human because it is more reticent to give a reason for all the evil and malice in the world: we simply have no rationally satisfactory, overall explanation for human suffering and for the many misfortunes we see every day (most of it in the media), and which sometimes strike us personally. Often, the only way we can endure inexplicable and (apparently?) absurd human suffering is by standing together; we can do what we can to ease people's pain, we can actively resist injustice, and we can trust in the "sym-pathy" of our God, who "feels for us". We recall that our God endured human suffering to the very last and experienced the shame of the cross. With this in mind we are privileged to hope that our utterly personal cross in this life will be followed by our individual resurrection beyond the frontier of death.

5. Bibliography

N. Bischofberger: Der Reinkarnationsgedanke in der europäischen Antike und Neuzeit, in: Die Idee der Reinkarnation in Ost und West. Munich 1996.

G. Gäde: Reinkarnation und Auferstehung. Zur Klärung des theologisch-epistemologischen Status. Überarbeitete und leicht erweiterte Fassung einer öffentlichen Probevorlesung im Rahmen eines Habilitationsverfahrens am 22.7.1997 vor der Katholisch-Theologischen Fakultät der Ludwig-Maximilians-Universität Munich.
http://www.gerhardgaede.de/uploads/media/Reinkarnation.pdf

M. Kehl: Und was kommt nach dem Ende? Von Weltuntergang und Vollendung, Wiedergeburt und Auferstehung. 3rd ed., Freiburg 2000, pp. 47 – 71:

F.-J. Nocke: Eschatologie II, in: Th. Schneider (ed.): Handbuch der Dogmatik Vol. 2, ppb-Ausgabe, Düsseldorf [2]2000, pp. 468 – 471.

R. Sachau: Westliche Reinkarnationsvorstellungen. Gütersloh 1996.

K. Rahner; H. Vorgrimler: Kleines Konzilskompendium. Freiburg [26]1994. p. 356 f.

W. Thiede: Warum ich nicht an Reinkarnation glaube. Ein theologischer Diskussionsbeitrag. EZW-Texte 1997, no. 136.

H. Zander: Geschichte der Seelenwanderung in Europa. Alternative religiöse Traditionen von der Antike bis heute. Darmstadt 1999.